TEXTS
FROM
LAST NIGHT

WTF
WTF

 + + XXX

TEXTS

FROM

ALL THE TEXTS
NO ONE REMEMBERS SENDING

LAUREN LETO AND BEN BATOR

GOTHAM
BOOKS

LAST

NIGHT

GOTHAM BOOKS
Published by Penguin Group (USA) Inc.
375 Hudson Street, New York, New York 10014, U.S.A.
Penguin Group (Canada), 90 Eglinton Avenue East, Suite 700, Toronto, Ontario M4P 2Y3,
Canada (a division of Pearson Penguin Canada Inc.); Penguin Books Ltd, 80 Strand, London
WC2R 0RL, England; Penguin Ireland, 25 St Stephen's Green, Dublin 2, Ireland (a division of
Penguin Books Ltd); Penguin Group (Australia), 250 Camberwell Road, Camberwell, Victoria
3124, Australia (a division of Pearson Australia Group Pty Ltd); Penguin Books India Pvt Ltd,
11 Community Centre, Panchsheel Park, New Delhi — 110 017, India; Penguin Group (NZ), 67
Apollo Drive, Rosedale, North Shore 0632, New Zealand (a division of Pearson New Zealand
Ltd); Penguin Books (South Africa) (Pty) Ltd, 24 Sturdee Avenue, Rosebank, Johannesburg
2196, South Africa

Penguin Books Ltd, Registered Offices: 80 Strand, London WC2R 0RL, England

Published by Gotham Books, a member of Penguin Group (USA) Inc.

First printing, January 2010
10 9 8 7 6 5

Gotham Books and the skyscraper logo are trademarks of Penguin Group (USA) Inc.
LIBRARY OF CONGRESS CATALOGING-IN-PUBLICATION DATA HAS BEEN APPLIED FOR.

ISBN 978-1-592-40543-5

Printed in the United States of America
Set in Walbaum
Designed and illustrated by Ben Gibson

While the author has made every effort to provide accurate telephone numbers and Internet
addresses at the time of publication, neither the publisher nor the author assumes any responsibility for errors, or for changes that occur after publication

INTRODUCTION

For those of you who don't know, we founded TFLN for reasons that include: Kwame Kilpatrick (our sexting ex-mayor of Detroit), old flings, law school, repeatedly closing down bars and leaving tabs open, and one night in an MGM hotel room.

Before that, we laughed and cried privately and among friends over the mishaps and misfires created by pressing the "send" button a little too liberally. Those fuzzy memories used to live on in our inboxes until we ran out of room or we hit "delete." Now they're immortalized forever in paperback—or at least until Sarah Palin organizes a book-burning party for us (we know it's coming).

We have deeply penetrated (heh) our database of more than one million text messages to find the best of the best for your reading pleasure.

Until next time: drink up, text away, and outwit those hangovers.

[LL: MY FAVORITE TEXTS]:

(805): before i could say "i'm not that kind of girl", i was.

(770): I got us kicked out of the bar because the waitress found me in the kitchen trying to make spaghetti

(503): I want to be a jewelry store heckler. "Hey man, is she really worth it"

(909): I framed a picture of a seagull shitting and hung it in my house. I'm waiting to see how long it takes everyone to notice.

(226): forecast for tonight is alcohol, low standards and poor decisions.

(310): This row in front of you is like duck, duck, goose—but eating disorder, eating disorder, failed eating disorder

(559): he only lasted three minutes, so to spite him i stayed the night and slept in.

(214): dude. I'm so drunk.

(972): pete, this is bryce's mom

(214): I can't wait to have my cock in your ass

(972): pete, this is still bryce's mom

(262): Hi, I just found this phone under my seat at a brewers game and seeing as you're entered in as 'fillllatio' I figured I'd ask you if you know the illiterate ass who owns this phone.

Thanks :)

(574): I just saw the dad from "Little People Big World" at the airport. I chased him down and congratulated him for beating the DUI.

(484): Just heard a guy discussing with someone else the amazing blow job you gave him. I'm in New York. Over 2 hours away from where you live. I have never been more proud.

(614): how to cook rice: 1. put random amount of rice and water in a pot 2. have sex on the kitchen floor. when you are done having sex the rice is ready

(904): When I asked if she spit or swallow she replied "I never learned how to spit"

(203): You were parading around the bar chugging girls drinks and then asking them if you could buy them a drink. It was actually genius

(214): She's leaving for college so I made her a gift basket with all the essentials. You know- Ramen, a 12 pack of PBR, some leftover Plan B pills and a laminated business card for a good lawyer. Damn I'm a good big sister.

(970): i take joy in having bigger boobs than others

(817): i love marijuana more then i could love a human baby.

(513): You were screaming at a bartender last night for not referring to you as god.
(513): and apparently I tried to pay for beer with a tampon.

(720): Just lost my virginity while listening to rick astley. torn between horror and jubilation

(807): discovery: the myth about swedish girls giving good head? not a myth.

(412): I think that i just found proof that harry and ginny had sex

(770): cant believe you said you would bone perez hilton
(1-770): i said paris hilton
(770): thats even worse

(215): Please dont use Danity Kane lyrics to describe your emotions.

(646): the couple across the street's about to bang. go get the popcorn and come join us.

(519): oh, and bring over your fire extinguisher. we're gonna get the mailman again

(612): Me too. I'd like to spend all next summer high and drunk and riding ponies and boys.

(507): We had to use the stains on Phil's shirt to try to piece together what happened last night.

(602): I'm pretty sure the new "vibrating mascara" is just a disguised dildo for those of us who are too ashamed to purchase a real one.
(623): Well, at least their eye lashes will look good while they masturbate shamefully.

(917): i got us presents.
or arrested.
we shall see!

(202): I was about to go down on her and her dong flopped out and hit me in the chin. This may have a Nam like post-traumatic-stress-disorder effect on me.

(561): i stole $50 bucks from my girlfriends purse to pay for my other girls abortion pill . . . shes gonna be pissed

(918): Vegas for my brothers bachelor party. Just landed and I have a boner. I'm giggly and teary eyed I'm so excited.

(978): highlight from tonight: i hit on her and her mother.

(225): If I die today, promise to let the world know I partied. . . . oh god did I party

(347): I knew you were gonna be a good wingman when the words "dibs on the chunky one" came out of your mouth.

(303): I have to decide between the hot young blond with no apparent gag reflex, and the brunette with a great ass and a trust fund.

(908): It was at that point the crowd that gathered realized i wasn't getting arrested, and passed the sobriety tests. I got a standing ovation from 25 strangers

(312): I remember going home with 2 girls. Woke up with 4.

(612): we're getting ready to take strippers to breakfast. I love my life.

(971): I have two black x marks on my hands.
(503): Yep you got cut off last night after a stripper bent over in front of you and you screamed very loudly 'I can see your soul from here'
(971): damnit I wish I could remember that.

(936): Whats contracted in vegas does not stay in vegas. . . .

(253): i wanted to iron the shorts i'm wearing. but i'm high and lazy. so i'm using my hair straightener. in bed.

(503): I'm sitting next to this guy at the bar. I wrote him a little song in my head it goes "there is no fucking chance you're getting in my pants" gonna sing it to him after he buys me another drink.

(734): I just met a guy from Australia at the bar. I asked him what it was like down under and he told me if I went home with him he'd let me find out. I love Australians.

(305): I may be the skinniest girl here. I like this crowd.

(704): Wearing these hooker shoes was a mistake

(828): proudest moment: just made a guy walk into a parked car with his mouth hanging open cause of the shirt im wearing.

(774): i just walked into a room at this party and someone yelled "dibs!"...

(214): Sex on bubble wrap = best decision ever.

(513): thought so. i woke up and he was playing with my eyeliner. I MAKE GREAT CHOICES.

(512): I just had to explain to the pharmacy cashier that the Plan B and thank you notes I was buying were not related

(423): NEED BACKUP we are in the kitchen arguing about who would win in fight against lil Wayne and snoop dog

(630): is it gross that my labia hangs so much that guys can't find my clit?

(404): He was so confused why there was a string hanging out of my vagina.

(902): I didn't notice until this morning that he had a six inch RAT TAIL . . .

(919): The chick I went home with last night had a happy trail

(813): Update: Discussing lingerie with my father. He likes sheer black things. Not into the colorful stuff I wear.

(949): Dood you jacked it to warcraft. you can't come back from something like that

(270): i'm the matthew mcconaghey of this party. i'm too old, and too high.

(412): He's gotten way too comfortable around me. He came into the bathroom and took a shit while I was in the shower.

(832): super hot butfun
(832): Oops. What a difference a comma and a space make.

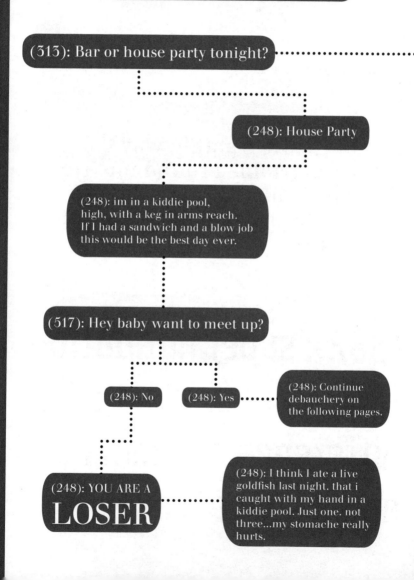

CHOOSE YOUR OWN BAD DECISIONS

(313): Bar or house party tonight?

(248): House Party

(248): im in a kiddie pool, high, with a keg in arms reach. If I had a sandwich and a blow job this would be the best day ever.

(517): Hey baby want to meet up?

(248): No

(248): Yes

(248): Continue debauchery on the following pages.

(248): YOU ARE A LOSER

(248): I think I ate a live goldfish last night. that i caught with my hand in a kiddie pool. Just one. not three...my stomache really hurts.

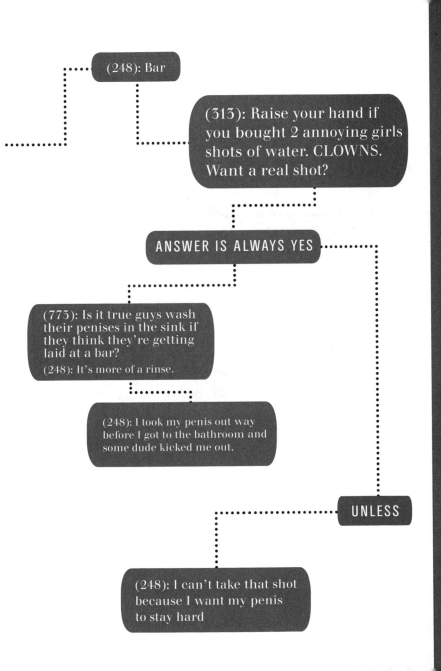

(248): Going to meet up with the girl

(313): Say my name once during sex just to fuck with her. Like when it gets rough.

(609): take another shot before he comes over?

IF NO

(313): How's it going

(248): I'm texting you during a blow job. She thinks I'm looking shit up. Ftw.

.......................➤ IF YES

(517): so i completely puked my brains out. a lot. he held me up so i could brush my teeth. then we proceeded to hook up for the next four hours.

(609): he's a keeper

(248): she just waddled down the stairs behind me and puked and kind of reached for me but i sped up. does that make me a bad person?

(513): why did they invent bidet's? your butt gets clean when your poop falls in the toilet and splashes up anyway . . .

(734): the whole time he was cumming, he did the joey lawrence WHOA. over and over. WHOA. WHOA. WHOA. WHOA.

(+44): Next time, if you wake and bake, make sure you nail the wake part. Not easy to explain to mum. Or the fire brigade.

(703): so he came on my face and then proceeded to say "that was just how i imagined it would happen"
(1-703): where do you find these guys?

(862): i was having this nice romantic moment with my girlfriend. then jimmy came in and peed on the fridge

(727): He just asked me if I ever had the urge to put a zucchini in my ass.

(972): 90% of the problems in your life are directly related to your vagina

(613): i have it on good authority that she is not as good at giving head as she claims she is

(970): If he comes back to you and I'm left alone in lonelytown I'm totally going to poo on your car.

(678): I read the police report. You asked the cop if you could use his in-car computer to update your facebook. No way you get out of a DUI.

(845): puked in the new house. now it's officially home.

(442): seems the shocker is way more shocking if u get the fingers wrong

(541): You told me that wouldnt happen if we used an enema before

(240): Banned from zoo.
(301): Again?

(571): I was getting a bj with sports center on in the background
(202): Da na na, na na naa

(860): What did we do last night that was yellow?

(915): i either bought an eighteen year old girl or i'm engaged to her . . . i'm not quite sure

(310): my mom just walked in on me furiously masturbating while reading twilight. needless to say, im officially out of the closet.

(650): Just FYI I rubbed poison oak on all your sheets and blankets so we all will know who you hooked up with (in about a day)

(516): the police officer looked at my vomit and told me "milk was a bad choice"

(313): so i woke up to her 8 year old asking for a bowl of cereal . . .

(310): you need to understand the magnitude of this. i just made margarita cupcakes.

(631): woke up naked, spooning with wine bottle.. and my video chat was still open. fuck, not again.

(908): ambulance drove by playing 'What Is Love?' on the loudspeaker. both driver and passenger were head bobbing.

(303): @ 711, condom and lube fall on floor. I don't notice. old lady taps me on shoulder 2 tell me. everyone looks. YES. that just happened

(506): drank two beers while on the toilet at home during lunch break. new high or new low, not sure

(416): I think my emotional moodswings have reached a new low. I cried for the entire duration of changing my tampon.

(650): just had a super intense, drunken debate about which blink182 member is the most fuckable. i got so mad i left the room. new low.

(909): College reaches a new low. We just carved a shot glass out of a potatoe.

(734): Gte hit a new low, I took a poopnap, passed out mid poop on the toilet.

(704): so i woke up with ketchup and a sticky boob on my face . . . this is a new low

(650): Just soaked up some whiskey with a paper towel and then squeezed it into a cup for consumption. New low.

(914): so now that im really awake i see that my underwear are completely ripped down the side, my shorts are on backwards, i have to go get plan b. . . . i call last night an epic fail or success depending on how catholic i am feeling

(301): do girls know yet that the best boners are in the morning?

(732): some girl had on jean underwear. i hate america.

(304): apparently smacking a customer in the face with his iPhone was not part of the WOW factor we learned in training . . .

(901): great sex! but now the fight over who sleeps on the wet spot starts.

(440): I went to the gynecologist and they said, "you're the most fun person we've ever had," and i thought, "that's exactly why i'm here!"

(952): You remember correctly you did get a golf cart ride out but it wasnt because you were special. You were so smashed you were screaming tiger at random golfers in the middle of there backswing.

(925): you told her you hoped she was a lawyer because she was too ugly to have a 'nice person' job.

(908): There's a guy next to me wearing a shirt that says "if you're happy and you know it grab my dick." i'm happy, so do i do it?

(208): he told me that by having sex with him it would be helping out his marriage.

(281): it was understandable until you starting crying because you missed "face" from nickelodeon

(512): Played the LOTR drinking game last night. Ended up in boxers running thru the lot at ross's place screaming "for frodo"

(505): My toast was "here's to being positive, and testing negative . . . Cheers!". . . after that chick gagged on her shot, everyone knew. . . . slut.

(773): i just turned Barefoot Contessa into a drinking game. everytime she uses a knife butter or salt i drink.

(503): i'm playing scrabble with my parents and i could totally win this game but it requires me to put 'cunt' down and i just can't do it.

(315): playing new game: drink everytime u see someone at the beach with a tramp stamp, double if u guess it before u see it, triple for male tramp stamps
(315): warning: blackouts possible when playing in ocean city or anywhere in new jersey

(908): we're taking shots every time my dog licks his penis. we're on number 8 now.
(1-908): you should have been aborted.

(517): every time you feel disappointed with the red wings take a shot

(404): Forget abc fam drinking games. Take a shot everytime Tyra says I and you'll be dead by the first commercial

**(802): last night i used 411 to try and contact britney spears.
(917): dollar well spent**

(480): the pyshco put "in a relationship bullshit" on facebook . . . this is not worth it
(206): watching you get rid of this one shall be very entertaining . . .

(815): someone called me shannon dorrhety annnd it hurt my feelingsd.

> (972): You can't fart with just two people. You need a third person to blame it on.

(212): it was a great night, didn't pay for anything
(914): the best nights you never pay for, except in dignity

(941): Do you think the doubletree will refund ourroom if we kindly explain to them that we all shacked elsewhere?

(248): I just beat a six year old at sorry . . . and im proud of myself

(360): I wish i could make my toaster dance like they do in the second ghostbusters. But i dont have ectoplasmic goo.
Or a toaster.

(908): google image searching george stephanopoulos at 1 AM on a saturday night . . . once again

(412): Just saw an old lady buying magnum condoms in giant eagle.
(1-412): did you applaud?

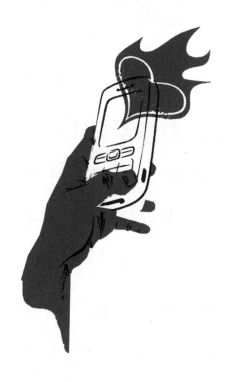

(802): does it bother you that i swallowed
like millions of your unborn children
(1-802): actually, i try not to think about it
(802): and i pooped them out

(850): Apparently last night I sat at the bar with an upside down sharpie lightning bolt on my forehead, yelling "It's Harry Potter's birthday! Let me be on the qudditch team!" And I kept calling the bartender Dobby. There are videos.

(616): Well looks like i have nothing better to do than find a secluded bathroom in the denver airport and trim my pubes

(630): i would rim the shit out of meg ryan

(712): Removable shower head + gerard butler singing "music of the night" + wine = amazing

(610): if you find a joe biden blowup doll in the attic, I call dibs

(845): I just decided that french people don't know/understand what they're saying to each other

(314): Yes. At Joey's but he said if you come he'll stab you with the spear in his basement

(289): i told her that Beatrice, the yogurt, was the widow of Tim Horton. and she believed me.

(714): Yes, I sucked on his balls. They tasted like Vienna Sausages dipped in tarter sauce.

(1-714): THIS IS YOUR BROTHER. I am going to need therapy.

(609): Our daughter's middle name will be Sangria. Do not attempt to fight me on this.
(1-609): I can't deal with this right now.
(609): CECELIA SANGRIA IS A BEAUTIFUL NAME.

(808): Sorry mate, forgive me. I'm doing stuff to your toothbrush again. Stuff with my penis.

(519): and then she said I drew a line on her forehead with my cum and whispered "Simba"

(608): You were saying you were peter pan and I was Tinkey Bell and you had to think happy thoughts, then you put your arms straight out and thought you were actually flying while the cab was moving.

(212): I'm in a subway station watching a tranny do her makeup. This is like watching a unicorn giving birth.

(951): who are the demons that keep, "According to Jim" on the air??

(214): I feel like a superhero. Should I use my new boobs for good or for evil?

(269): No one ever told me oral sex incorporated me licking her pee hole!

(814): Maybe she just tucks it between her legs every time you see her naked.

(212): I know she is the girl of my dreams bc she orgasmed, rolled over and then asked if I knew that Orlando beat Cleveland.

(612): You think the Elephant Man ever tried to pick up chicks claiming all his appendages were elephant-sized?

(762): Do you think the new Crest Whitestrips Advance Seal would stay on while I give him head? It would be great to knock out 2 things at once . . .

(818): So I answered the door in my underwear expecting my boyfriend. Instead I opened the door to Mormon missionaries. Do you think that was a sign from God?

(201): Do you ever think God made girls unattractive around their periods as a warning?

(608): Do you think people stop being hipsters when they're naked? because that's what my research shows.

(805): do you think they make care bear costumes for cats?

(732): Philosophical question: how many blocks away from the office do I need to be able to order a cocktail with lunch? Ps remind me to tell you about my left nipple.

(256): ever wondered if the dollar in your wallet has ever been in a stripper's butt crack?

(603): You think if I promise to behave for the rest of my life, god will let me fuck her on the regular?

(404): My phone didn't know the word "conscience," do you think that is indicative of something?

(620): Do you think there's anyone left in this world that hasn't masturbated in a computer chair?

(402): Bar closing I am hiding in the bathroom. do you think anyone will find me?

(216): my tampon string is in my asshole . . . do you think i can get it out without anyone noticing?
(1-216): i'd get off the bar first.

(985): Don't you think facebook is a bit pretentious, suggesting friends and all? No facebook, I would NOT like to be friends with a girl whose fiance I have slept with.

(410): Do you think if I drink bleach they will let me leave work?

(515): Do you think Capital One would let me put the Tub Girl picture on my Capital One card?

(847): Beat you to it.

(818): do you think pornstars masturbate to their own videos?

(304): Do you think fat gay guys titty fuck?

(1-304): I haven't heard from you in over a month and that's what you come with?

(772): So they call it the mile high club when you have sex on a plane. What do you think they call it if you fuck a just fired stripper on a greyhound bus?

(812): Is it weird that I think of Ennis from Brokeback Mountain everytime I hear "Make Em' Say Uhh!" by Master P? "I don't need your money. Huh." NA NA NA NAAA.

(631): all I know is if I don't watch spice world right now there will be a firefight.

(480): The producers of Marley and Me owe me about $5 million. That's the dollar amount of embarrassment compensation required for making a 24-year-old male cry publicly on an airplane while sitting in the middle seat between a gorgeous babe and a guy with a do-rag

RELATIONSHIP TIMELINE

First Meeting

(414): hey, we just made out in the backyeard. i'm inside now and you should come to the bathroom and meet me.

First Night Together

(517): he confessed his love for me, threw up on my pillow and then fell asleep on said pillow. i met him last night.

(231): better than last weekend. things are really looking up for you.

First Date

(516): Make note: the first date is too soon to make the "condoms are only for making balloon animals" joke.

First Fight

(845): maybe if you didn't yell 'buh duh duh da duh da dats all folks' when you came she wouldn't have left last night

First Time Letting It Go

(719): just survived the first fart of the relationship.

First Time Meeting the Parents

(770): I just barfed on his mom.
(404): You told him you were too drunk to meet his parents. Totally his fault.

First Sign of a Long-Term Relationship

(662): I can't believe you blew on her face.
(1-662): I feel that every long term relationship needs at least one big,load delivered straight between the eyes.

First Breakup

(773): I accidentally broke up with him while I was drunk which is really too bad since I'd just gotten a birth control prescription so we could start having sex.

(773): Do you think he'd take me back if I said "dude, we need to get back together or this IUD is going to have an existential crisis for not realizing its full potential"?

First Makeup

(630): but it happened after you broke up with me and before we made up.

Second Breakup

(503): he broke up with me so i peed in his bed

First Rebound

(415): JACOB AND UGLY BROKE UP

First Time Seeing Each Other Again

(803): It was good seeing you tonight, I'm glad we could be cordial around eachother

(912): "butterface", "the bitch from hell" and "crazy fuck" is how our table referred to you. It was great seeing you as well.

(704): You know the commpass Jack Sparrow has? The one that just points at whatever you want? Thas pretty much my moral compass.

(570): She's like the female version of the Memento guy. She keeps forgetting that I'm an asshole after we have sex.

(212): I just watched Juno. I kind of wish I was in highschool and pregnant

(850): It wasn't awkward until he started humming the Rocky theme song in the middle of fucking

(219): community service is like the breakfast club . . . except we're all the criminal.

(202): I tried to gradually lead her into my room but she wouldn't stop crying and quoting memoirs of a geisha

(603): Is it a little weird that I have a ridiculous urge to have sex while the theme song to the Pirates of the Carrbibbean blares in the background?

(203): I woke up this morning and "The Wood" was on tv. Touche TBS, touche.

(540): what do you have against ST
(1-540): DO NOT ABBREVIATE LIKE YOU AND STAR TREK ARE FRIENDS.

(828): All time low . . . just gave a strip tease to the theme song from Law&Order SVU.

(804): So how Liz Lemon is this? I bring a boy home, we get in bed, and I realize there's a lean pocket wrapper in the sheets.

(616): this girl looks like the female version of brooke hogan

(251): How was last night?
(334): She looked like Delta Burke in her fat Designing Women days . . . and she just left like 2 minutes ago. Right after breakfast.

(703): Please advise as to how precisely ashamed I should be if I just became sexually aroused by a Harry Potter and the Half Blood Prince preview

(617): yo I sort of want to fuck rachel maddow. but I'm not a lesbian. actually I reaally want to so maybe I am a lesbian. at least on weekdays at 9.

(859): What I dont get about To Catch a Predator is who the fuck still uses chat rooms?

(780): Girls gone wild is like the hills, except sexy and it doesnt suck

(630): 8th day he invented the big mac, 9th he invented pop rocks, 10th day boobs.

(217): i just google searched "what time does taco bell open"

(619): no more stoned jack in the box. this is the third night in a row.

(706): i would punch a child for taco bell

(918): Just saw a policeman use his lights to go through a red light only to turn them off and go to Sonic . . .

(919): I just had to pull over at a starbucks to throw up in the bathroom. They really should not have let me be a lawyer.

(573): i left the bar a little after you and ended up flipping my car in the arbys drive thru

(404): A little girl and i are having a face making battle in mcdonalds
(404): She started it, but I totally finished it.

(847): just took a sink shower in Arbys bathroom

(301): is it bad that the cashier at chick-fil-a shouted "see you tomorrow!" as i drove away?

(704): We're pre-gaming then going to chuck e cheese's.
(919): If you're joking I'm going to be sad

(405): Assholes at mcdonalds drive through wouldn't serve us last night even though we said we were on small motorcycles that were to small for them to see and weren't heavy enough for the sensors. We made noises and everything.

(334): you should have seen this little asian lady pumping the shit out of the arby sauce pump. it was hot and she was smiling and so into it. she was so old and horny.

(937): My armpits smell like big macs again. I think I need new deodorant.

(818): Just saw a hooker at Wendy's who loudly supported public urination and cut in front of me while possibly muttering something about a "white devil." I was going to say something, but that just wasn't a fight I was going to win.

(407): Peeing in a burger king cup while driving on the highway = a lot easier than i expected

(250): i'm listening to "Transmission" by The Tea Party from like '97 and waxing my legs. fuck i'm awesome in my alone time

(507):

drinking colt 45 because lando calrissian told me to

**(843): the red head has a bf
(1-843): just because there's a goalie doesn't mean u can't score**

(904): im marching my happy ass in there and im not leaving until he cheats on his girlfriend!

(808): The funny thing about my wife cheating on me is that the guy probably has genital warts now. Sweet.

(434): u cheatin on me?
(1-434): if i did i would try to upgrade babe.

(510): The party tonight has no theme but I decided to go as a home wrecker.

(757): this guy asked for my number but didn't have paper to write it down, so he went to write it on his hand i saw he also had the word "diapers" written.

(314): I accidentally told him I've been cheating on him with his brother last night.

(540): I just crawled out of a second story window using a sheet and his clothes for a rope so he wouldn't wake up.
(540): I am so glad I watched Macgyver as a kid.

(678): why did i wake up with a kid named Raphael in my bed this morning?
(770): I dont know but you did call last night to tell me you found the last ninja turtle

(803): im on my way to getting "i just graduated college with no money, no job, and no plan" drunk

(830): If I was Danny Tanner and my wife died and left me with three kids I would hire a nanny rather than bringing in the sexually promiscuos uncle with a fetish for leather and rebellion and my obviously mentally ill (possibly gay) best friend Joey, who has never had a girlfriend and consistently talks in cartoon voices . . . a nanny is just a better choice

(202): therell be strippers and coke right?
(703): no strippers. just coke.
(202): i hate this fuckin recession

(818): searching for a job in this recession is like trying to find the clit. i'm screwed

(949): Bro, did you remember the lagoon creature you hooked up with last nite?
(1-949): We're in a recession man

(301): i kept saying "bloody hell" in a ron weasley accent until i forcibly told myself to shut up

(708): i felt like we were having sex on Ultimate Fighter, and people on the outside kept yelling ELBOW ELBOW! KNEES KNEES!

(619): I think I kinda wanna bone that ginger from Harry Potter.
(1-619): You literally just made my flesh crawl.

(864): weed, chlorine, and victory. my bed smells like i had sex with michael phelps.

(847): And God said, "Let there be Twilight," and it was so.
(1-847): I should injure you considerably.

(815): It was about as enjoyable as phone sex with Diane Rehm

(859): he asked me if i knew what a blumpkin was . . . i shouldnt have agreed to find out before he told me the definition.

(720): It was awkward until we both realized our obsessions with harry potter and sangrias were the same. Now were in love.

(920): You need to get a life and stop texting me about fictional characters. I don't give a shit.

(303): maybe i would like her more if 99% of her sentences didn't start with "yesterday when i was reading Twilight . . .

(410): he is naked. in. my. bed. happiest day. of my. LIFE.

(970): You were telling me about how you were gonna marry him, have his children and name them all woodchip.

(917): My milkshake brings 85 to 90 percent of the boys to the yard

(917): I'm once again drinking at eight am on a Sunday in my tutu. This garment is literally my best purchase ever.

(360): So I don't have any furniture but we just skateboard drunk around the floor.

(631): Morgan Freeman can narrate your sex life and it still wouldn't interest me.

(803): I bet the first caveman to make fire got so much pussy

(818): Its about making memories worth repressing

(508): Don't go all Obama on me. George Bush this decision and just do it. Thinking's for the morning after

(201): you told everyone your name was brenda and you had the whole party chanting b-dawgg by the end of the night. successful.

(239): I wish I could drop acid with the muppets

(870): I don't get it.

(501): Me neither.

(501): But I masturbated to it anyway.

(702): I wish we could go back in time and find our best farts ever

(604): it was beautiful and magic like when a hot girl grabs her own tits and smiles at you

(484): I totally just used John Mayer's lyrics to get laid.

(301): i wanna do a homemade sex video in sepia and pretend were in the early 20th c

(262): I am engaged

(262): To a real live girl that has met me

DEATHS FROM LAST NIGHT

[NATASHA RICHARDSON (MAY 11, 1963–MARCH 18, 2009)]:

(512): I hit my head so hard last night drunk swimming at 430am that I thought i was gonna die in my sleep like Natasha Richardson. I went as far as to write a note that said, "MOM GETS EVERYTHING." I found my 'will' this morning on a napkin covered in Easy Mac cheese sauce and pepperoni cubes. You missed a good time last night

[DAVID CARRADINE (DECEMBER 8, 1936–JUNE 3, 2009)]:

(312): office poll is still running 100% that Spencer Pratt is more disturbing than David Carradine's death

[ED MCMAHON (MARCH 6, 1923–JUNE 23, 2009)]:

(570): I'm going Ed McMahoning tonight.

(610): What?

(570): I'm going to spend all my money and die. . . . too soon?

[FARRAH FAWCETT (FEBRUARY 2, 1947–JUNE 25, 2009) AND MICHAEL JACKSON (AUGUST 29, 1958–JUNE 25, 2009)]:

(325): I bet farrah fawcett is having words with michael jackson in heaven for stealing her thunder

[BILLY MAYS (JULY 20, 1958-JUNE 28, 2009)]:

(972): they say celebs die in threes. leave it to billy mays to throw in one extra COMPLETELY FREE!

[STEVE MCNAIR (FEBRUARY 14, 1973-JULY 4, 2009)]:

(717): you know how mcnair got capped

(717): my first reaction was 'why couldnt it have been mcnabb'

(215): omg you bastard

[WALTER CRONKITE (NOVEMBER 4, 1916–JULY 17, 2009)]:

(614): We were so high you accused Luke of faking Walter Cronkite's death and selfishly using him to narrate his life.

[JOHN HUGHES (FEBRUARY 18, 1950–AUGUST 6, 2009)]:

(847): john hughes is dead. crushing any and all dreams of me ever being in an '80s john hughes film. bummer.

[TED KENNEDY (FEBRUARY 22, 1932–AUGUST 25, 2009)]:

(508): Ted Kennedy liked long drives on short bridges

$\Big[$ DOMINICK DUNNE
(OCTOBER 29, 1925-AUGUST 26, 2009) $\Big]$:

(718): OMG having a crisis, Dominick Dunne died and i just learned he wasn't gay!!! AGAIN OMG!

$\Big[$ ADAM GOLDSTEIN (MARCH 30, 1973-AUGUST 28, 2009) $\Big]$:

(541): I just hope this isn't happening Final Destination style

(1-541): Travis Barker would totally be Devon Sawa in this scenario

(404): i hope kanye doesn't show up to patrick swayze's funeral. "I'll let you get back to your funeral in a minute . . . but michael jackson had the best death of the year. just sayinnn"

(904): He had a number 3 tattooed on his penis And when I asked what it meant, he said "you know like dale earnhardt, the intimidator"

(570): Let's make love on the newspapers that declare financial doomsday

(781): Fucking love it maybe bedazzle some baby seals? Make them cuter? Who would club a bedazzled baby seal? Only a fucking monster.

> (703): Whenever I'm sad I just imagine if babies were born with mustaches . . .

(434): why are there goldfish crackers all over my bed?
(540): you decided you wanted to name them & keep them as pets.

> (717): hey this is lauren, i have to type for jon because he's convinced the tongs he's holding are his real hands

(815): I met the nicest Tranny last night. He/She loves Cheetos.

(303): It smells like weed.
(720): We are in Boulder, Everything smells like weed.

(559): Just figured out how to smoke weed with a toaster.

(503): what has become of my life if the best thing thats happened to me this week is that i discovered my cleavage as the best hiding spot ever for weed.

(704): I got so high last night I started crying because i couldn't stop thinking about how scary space is

(661): I just rolled a spliff on a dora the explorer tv tray. Preschool education meet afterschool special.

(407): so the weed I found in my fridge is actually lettuce. tell jim I need that 5 bucks after all

(804): the power's out. i'm smoking weed by flashlight
(1-804): i wish i was dedicated to anything like you are to weed

(770): honestly, who buys weed with an unemployment check?
(1-770): you.
(770): oh yeah. preciate

(512): my dad just secretly slid me a nugg in front of my mom. remind me why I moved away for college??

(855): I am at a 420 party and i just told a girl "hey, less not getting donuts, more getting donuts"
(1-855): and did she get any doughnuts?
(855): No. I am devastated

(408): i'm so high i feel like the people i'm chatting with online can some how see that i'm naked.

(404): I hate seeing commercials about babies when i'm high
(954): Yeah, I don't like babies at all

(909): dude i'm inner monologue high

(561): As a matter of fact my bong is named Hulkamania brother

(805): i can totally tell he's high. he's having a conversation with my dog.

(919): so I was just driving high and I stopped to let a pinecone cross the road because I thought it was a hedgehog.

(416): i have a strong urge to join the asians in the park doing tai chi. I think im still high.

(721): That guy over there looks like a cartoon/action figure.
(703): omg, i know.
(721): we're too high.

(973): On a scale from 0 to 24 . . . wait, 3 to 24, where 6 is the lowest and 12 is the highest, how freaking high re you right now?

(952): When are you coming home?
(715): When the phone isn't in 3D.

(714): so i ate the brownie and i don't feel any high at all. i did however just eat 6 slices of pizza though, which i find amazing . . .

(386): i wish we had vans that drove around at night but instead of ice cream and jolly tunes its taco bell and the macarena

(651): theres bread in your mailbox im going to eat it
(651): nevermind its newpaper

(925): i just had a dream that i could control how black Will Smith was with a remote.i need to stop sleeping with the TV on

(504): Tickle wars 95% of the time end in sex.

(617): i wanna stay in my bed and fart for a few more hours

(781): I've decided that life's journeys are more fun when your moral compass hangs in front of you and swings with each step

(603): all we need is a shotglass and a helicopter.

(202): Haha so apparently that girl last thought I was you the whole time, and in the morning realized you weren't the one she fucked. Thanks for your help.

(650): my vag is singing 'hurts so good' by john mellencamp

(334): I'm think I may have given your ex's number to a convicted sex offender.
(205): Win!

(865): dude, that chick is coming to see me and stay for 2 nights. I'm hitting the 3rd in the trifecta of friends.
(302): You're one hell of a depraved bastard dude, I'm borderline speechless. You officially win.
(865): They all have matching tattoos so they're all official bffs. I love my life.

(502): The best thing happened. Some guy was butchering Conway Twitty at karaoke and the power went off in the whole bar. And someone shouted "you pissed jesus off when you messed with conway!"

(323): If I ever start a band I'm gonna name it "Nancy Reagan's Vagina"

(305): Thanks for jumping on that grenade for me last night. You're the best wingman ever
(615): She ate 7 of the 8 slices of pizza. I deserve a purple heart and sex w your sister

(405): Dude, I'm in her bathroom and there's crab shampoo . . . is it worth the risk?
(918): You're missing what this discovery implies . . . she's got a fucking bush.
(405): I wish there were wingman of the year awards.

(417): true best friends attempt to put quarters in each others butts. Thanks for the best birthday ever!

(202): I hid a 6pack in the microwave for later
(410): I knew I liked you

(484): Quick-how do i get carpet marks off my knees in like 5 mins?

(210): Dude why does my asshole itch so bad?
(1-210): I'll teach you how to wipe better

(719): I passed out in Idaho and woke up in Washington vomiting into my roommate's fishbowl. The fish was on the floor.
(719): Don't worry, I took the fish out first.

(908): But i did once see a show where a women was homeless and installed a stove in a school bus so she and her baby could live there since all the seats were taken out. As far as being homeless goes it didn't look half bad . . . So this is me promising to you that if i ever am living in an abandoned school bus . . . i will at least pimp it out with a stove so you can come over for dinner sometimes

(913): My favorite part of our friendship is your tits.

847): he kept farting in my kitchen and blaming it on the dog. then we went to wendy's and he spent twenty minutes in the bathroom. im pretty sure he shit his pants.
(1-847): you should have known when you found out he drove a mini cooper not to hang out with him.

(615): Apparently I farted on her in my sleep. Then, just to be sure she was cool, I did it again on purpose and she didnt say anything. So, WIN?

(856): I just farted so loud that my cat got so scared he fell off the couch.

(678): I was just at the urinal, started to go, then farted, then said oh yea out loud, then heard someone move in the stall behind me

(570): Babe! I just farted and I swear to jesus lord christ that it sounded like ur name! Ok, more like Meeatt but still . . . awesome.

(408): she farted while i was going down on her. not doing that again

(614): You're boyfriend is farting in his sleep. The last one sounded like a threat.

(203): I think my fart just growled at me.

(773): Let's start a violent farting gang. We can do walkbys.

(513): Dude, the girl next to me just farted. Worst part, it smells like astroglide

(847): I just tried to drunkenly fart the beat of Disturbia by Rihanna

(804): You can tell a man will be prosperous by the power of his farts- A fart that can shake the room is a voice that can change the world.

(425): my ass just sighed. even my farts are tired.

(913): So she farted while we were having sex but I was afraid she would stop because she was emberessed so i just went ahead and took the blame and apologized

(478): wow, farting in latex pants is really awkward.

(902): and then I told her I was too drunk. She started to cry, and told me this always happens to her and that she thinks shes ugly. I pretended I was asleep and then she farted.

(805): My farts woke her up so I pretended to be keep sleeping.

(310): im at the bar and i misjudged a fart . . . go home or ride the night out?Never mind, the bouncer made the decision for me . . . be home soon

(617): dude we were spooning naked in bed with her ass in my crotch. she sharted in her sleep all over my dick.

(757): Cool, see you soon . . . she just admitted to her friends that it was a queef.

(479): I didn't know that people actually queef. Is this a real thing?
(1-479): I believe so, yes.
(479): Would you be offended if I asked if it has happened to you?

(206): he needs to stop telling all his friends what my queefs sound like. its getting awkward to be around people who can quote my vagina.

(914): i'm in the sorta mood where i wanna be that crying, drunk girl who will hook up with anyone that tells her she's pretty

(865): we were having sex in the bathroom when his aunt knocked on the door
(865): and rather than go out and meet her, i climbed out the window. so now she thinks he was masturbating and moaning his own name in a really girly voice

(619): I like sleeping in my bed after you spend the night because the covers smell like you
(1-619): Luckily they don't smell like your farts.

(402): I shaved my pubes to make my cock look like it has a lions mane. to surprise the girl that works at the zoo when she comes over.

(419): Want to have sex later?
(614): This feels like a trap

(352): I either just heard my neighbors having sex or she really agreed with whatever he was talking about.

(504): My balls are about to become a huge part of your mouth's life

(301): i just dont know how to see an unattractive person as more than a friend

> (319): Decided to write a book called "girls don't poop and other myths I wish I still believed in"

(415): thank god random hookups don't end with college. happy birthday, america.

> (415): No, I'm a firm believer in "Swallow or it isn't love."

(251): Could you imagine if a Skynet machine combination of Bob Ross and Chuck Norris were built? It would rule the universe with a soft spoken fan brush of kung fu dominance
(303): It would be truly incredible. I hope we are blessed with this being in our lifetime.

> **(919):** i literally forgot his name and just started calling him "waffles"

(323): Ok pretty sure I just saw Mike O'Malley walking through the parking lot. I wanted to see if I followed him, would he lead me to the agro-crag, i've always wanted a crack at that bitch.

(253): My goal for the party is to get everyone in a diaper. Reasonable?

(705): "The real world" DC house is on the corner of 20th and S. Wanna come with to check it out? It's my goal to be a blurred out face in their hot tub.

(561): I wish there were whore gnomes that cleaned our apartment when we were gone.

(920): She just texted me saying, "I wish you were a better person so I could fuck you without regrets"

(864): sometimes i wish i was able to text my cat and tell him i miss him and that i'm thinking about him

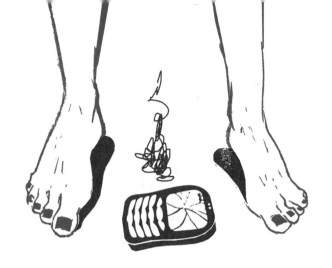

(775): i wish mother nature was an actual person cause i'd bitch slap her for sure

(214): I wish you were here to vomit in your hand.

(901): I really wish I could go back in time to change the course of events that led to me sitting on the internet at 3 Googling 'Traumatic masturbation' while talking to you about failed dates, and running a virtual restaurant in a video game.

(407): i went to disney world today with my friends, met snow white, then saw her later at a bar. she is naked next to me in her bed, passed out. when you wish upon a star . . .

(205): I just wish we had the ability to download food from our TVs.

(703): I wish I could be a nicer person. Or a more sober one.

(586): I wish my penis had an off switch

(509): My dream in life is to scissor with Ellen. I don't care if I've got a dick. I'll make it work.

(917): East Village: Only place you can play pac man while eating a pineapple hotdog, go to the bar next door and see a graphic blowjob on every tv

(914): I just came out of my doctor's office and i look into the window and i see a guy sitting in the front seat getting head.
(917): why are you so shocked? you live in brooklyn.

(718): I think getting shot is the thing to do in Brooklyn

(914): he puts the penis in happiness.

(914): he invited me to an all week drinking party at his house. apparently he knows the key to my heart is booze shaped.

(847): Journey is playing on the radio. . . . I think it is a sign I am going to pass my drug test

(815): yeah well you didn't even puke from the alcohol. we cut you off and went to huck finn's and told you that the "irish cream" coffee creamers had baileys in it, so you shot down like eight of them and puked all over the floor. it was great. we cheered you on and everything.

(312): she is unbelievable! ever pee on a girl?
(1-312): not while she was awake

(780): Is Jonathan Taylor Thomas a gay? I need you to google search it for me. Its imwportant

(773): Dude im not sure whos apartment i woke up in but i just showered here and their shampoo in phenomenal

(312): Who would have guessed that ordering a vodka lemonade at Roscoe's was code for I want a hand job

(848): life lesson #1: a fart during an awkward silence between 2 strangers doesnt make it less awkward.

(253): Life Lesson Number 76: Masturbating into a sock is useless if there is a hole in it.

> (678): Life lesson: if you fart while talking to a girl outside, the smell does not dissipate, it just lingers around mocking you

(678): Lesson learned: don't hide your vodka in your little brothers toy box.

(206): Tip for today: never try to fart and swallow at the same time. You'll end up choking on whatever you are currently swallowing and shit yourself from the freakout of choking.

(843): Tip #47, don't trim the bush when you have the shakes!

(647): fun fact: cucumber in vinegar with pepper = best ever high snack

(201): Note to Self: No matter how horny, turned on or in the moment you are, never go down on your gf after she had soccer practice.

(601): Here's my recipe for happiness. Go get a pen. 1. smoke a bowl 2. put on "explosions in the sky" 3. take a bath. Do this for about 1 hour or until all your problems go away.

(336): Note to self: When getting ready to leave with a kid in a wheelchair don't say Let's roll

(540): Note to self. Never fart in a tanning bed

(443): My mom came into my room and told me to flip off the tv. I gave it the middle finger. Note to self: STOP SMOKING THIS SHIT

(847): i just walked outside for a cigarette and three men walked by in glitter heels and gold shiny thongs. god i love chicago

> (650): i just saw a homeless guy running after a pigeon, catch it and put it in his jacket pocket. I'm not sure if the bird is now his pet or dinner!
> (408): Omg. Well, welcome to Oakland . . .

(510): You want to go to a white party at LAX
(1-510): Clubs are lame especially themed ones. Im not in a fucking episode of laguna beach

> (323): I would do things to you that would get us burned at the stake if we lived in a puritan village.

(323): Booty call?
(310): Dude you don't even follow my twitter

(323): Do you think an esthetician would be willing to wax the Chanel Cs into my crotch? That way, whenever a guy gets ready to pound on it I can go "Careful, it's Chanel."

(650): apparently i ate an entire bag of goldfish, kissed some guy with a girlfriend who now wants to kill me, made my sister sleep in my bed with me while i wore no pants, and told my whole family i am pregnant with jonny's devil baby . . . never drinking again

(415): If only Ben were 51% gay instead of 49%

(415): Dude, I just had an awesome rave/orgy with like bunch of hot Asian chicks on a cable car. It was like being in a Gwen Stefani video, cept w/o the bad spelling
(415): God, I love San Francisco

(408): carls jr on main st. japanese tourist taking a dump in the urinal. reading a japanese newspaper and wearing a full suit.
(415): be there in 3 mins

(650): Different chick, same blowjob, same parking lot.

(202): also, you're talking to the girl for whom "deformed baby arm" wasn't quite a dealbreaker.

(732): You know, Peter Parker would not have been nearly as cool if he had gotten bitten by an ant.

(202): respond to me or i'm telling everyone that you inserted a vodka soaked tampon into your anus

(202): Do ugly people know they are ugly?
(1-202): The quiet ones do.

(202): I just hatefucked a Bush administration appointee. Now having celebratory mimosas.

(202): i threw up in a trash can last night at kellys irish times. but in a trash can because i'm a lady

(202): you were definitelymotorboating random chicks as they walked out of the bar. just like, down the line. you kept yelling "Motor Boats for everyone!!!!"

(404): Made out with some random "plus sized" young lady. She let me kiss her boobies. It was like I was 6 months old again.

(404): I don't wanna do a drive in or see a movie tonight. I wanna play some Golden Tee and butt fuck a girl in the bathroom of some bar and proceed with Golden Tee

(770): Dear Mark, please dispose of your crusty mcdonalds napkins used to jerk it at my desk
(678): discrete masturbation is a lost art

(678): I have said "that's the wrong hole" for the last time.

(770): I gave her the chance to be interesting and she failed. So then I gave her a chance to be slutty and she failed at that too.

(404): Should I go home with him even though I know my Run DMC undies have skid marks on them?

(724): so i saw this homeless guy this morning yelling at a pay phone like chewbacca.
(412): That's what you get for being in filth-adelphia.

(215): how the fuck does easy mac keep making itself at 3am when i'm wasted? what is this phenomenon?

(215): i keep telling myself in the mirror "get undrunk"

(215): I swear if I see one more guy in a v-neck and fedora I'm going to punch someone in the balls. This is philly, you're not supposed to look like Ryan Cabrera

(206): We just picked up about 540 lbs of women. . . .

(206): Too bad my picture didn't come thru. It was one of me naked riding a unicorn with a wizard hat and a magic staff. And the unicorn had wings. And me too.

(206): I thought I was riding a bike, butI guess it was a vacuum cleaner

(206): Yes, one should always join a cult. At least once.

(206): This is your Morning Wood Report: I have it.

(360): If you're ever in Seattle we should Fuck. Or get coffee, whatever.

(360): The weather is perfect in Seattle right now. Warm enough for girls to not wear bras, but cold enough for me to see them nipping out in the shade.

(818): Also. Dude you have an iPhone "u" is not appropriate.

(770): The iPhone is ruining my ability to sex message. My 5-year-old cousin just picked up my phone at my grandmas birthday party and read "I wanna stand you up and fuck you from behind" to my entire extended family bc of popped up on my screen

(801): how do you clear previous safari searches on an iPhone? i asked my brother to google something for me and "big penis" "empire chinese food" and "reverse cowgirl" popped up.

(218): Sorry for the John Mayer like serenade I left on your phone last night. And sorry for the 3 other attempts because I didn't think it sounded right.

(251): Is there a "Plan B" app for my iphone?

(503): hey so do you know of any pussy modeling jobs?
(503): PUPPY. i meant puppy sorry

(281): How do you jack off and text at the same time?
(1-281): On my iPhone they have an app for that

(703): Blackberries need to come with a feature that disables texting to certain numbers after 2am based on content. like disabling texting to 'dad' containing the words 'lets try to find more blow.'

(857): seriously iPhone. stop autocorrecting all my fucks into ducks. you're making all my strong worded texts look harmless and adorable.

(734): Pissed on my Blackberry at the Astros game. Wish me luck explaining that one at work.

(254): I am coming home for anal
(254): *a nap*

(858): in retrospect, sexting while high was a mistake—I meant to say "I'll fuck you stupid, baby" but of course I said "I'll fuck your stupid baby"

(303): I just accidently sent "my poop smells like vodka" to 27 people in my phone book

(216): you sent me 5 happy birthday texts last night. one after the other. spelled differently.

(541): Words i added to my t9 today: gnomes, facebook, and chlamydia.

(810): My t9 writes chubies instead of bitches.
(1-810): either way. win, win.

(831): 'hiiiigh' is saved in my t9 for a reason

(602): Goodnight sugar queer
(480): Sugar queer??
(602): Why does my predictive text prioritize 'queer' over 'puffs'?

(425): dude, i'm now gay
(425): i mean 'not'

(519): I just accidentally send a text meant for you to this girl i was trying to hook up with saying, "I just got cockblocked by her cousin in the most effective way possible." Her cousin just died.

(214): would you ever date a girl who drove an 89 Chrysler LeBaron?—for the record it's a convertible

(214): The shirt is mine, the pants are mine, the bra not so much

(972): Don't feel obligated to get back to me but I think I just fell in love with a middle aged waitress at the Dennys in waco. She's used but in good condition.

(847): So I used to make fun of texas a lot, then I got here and I found a place where I could get my tequila in a to go cup with a straw and I realized that this is the only place I ever want to be

(469): Confirm your location. A cross street is best, but if google mapping yourself is your least-shameful option go for it. ps- going through his mail for an actual address is always an option.

(740): Please tell me how I woke up out in the middle of nowhere wearing nothing but a hard hat and a man thong?

(740): ran into someone who graduated hs with us while i was paying for booze in quarters. i love it when people from my past catch me in my classier moments.

(740): Baton twirling is one of his activities on facebook.
(740): Also he is "an Ohio Stae grand champion twirler". You cannot tell me he's straight

(740): Just saw an old lady trip and stumble. Laughed. Kept Driving. I'm going to hell.

(740): Dude there are two smokin hot chicks laying outside my apartment . . . I almost want to tell them theyre laying where I threw up last night
(631): U should. Its a good ice breaker

(740): the best things in life are free. have that freshly fucked look and doing the walk of shame by HIS girlfriend . . . priceless

(901): After he came all over my face, he proceeded to give me a high five. I can't even act upset because I always put myself in these situations. Did I mention D3: Mighty Ducks was playing in the background?

(204): I see an opportunity for you to use your nakedness to cure my boredom.

(403): So my grandma sent me a doily for my birthday—don't ask why, I don't know. Anyways I put my bong on it, I think it actually classed up the joint.

(403): My nephew just came out playing with my moms vibrator.

(954): you kept singing the copa cabana and saying HAVE A BANANA to random people on the street. you also went up to this poor short guy and hugged him while proceeding to yell I LOVE YOU CHILD MAN into his face. please tell me you're sober now

(850): Are they still out there making out on the couch? How can we get them to leave?
(850): I'm gonna go stand naked in the kitchen with a knife

(330): Fat strippers do more and I don't care who knows it.

(815): let's have some freedom sex
(630): i don't love our country that much

(952): So it turns out she's 40 and has a 20yo daughter.
(763): Do you still want to do her?
(952): I'd rather nail her daughter now.

(303): woke up next to a random this morning, pointed and said "stranger danger", he did not find it funny

(516): lets give the bartender the bail money in case they lock us both up for this.

(650): I woke up today, looked in the mirror, and said "Today, I don't give a fuck who sees my penis."

(917): Memory from last night that just came back: me forcibly jacking him off while he yelled I DONT LIKE HANDJOBS I DONT LIKE HANDJOBS

(832): I think we should go ahead and pin a note to my shirt when we go out that says "do NOT buy me shots"

(832): On the back we can put possible side effects may include: indiscriminate making out, brief crying spells, yelling in jibberish, and sudden sleep.

(970): I'm at a crab and wine festival with my dad. He just introduced me as his girlfriend to all of his co-workers. I am so drunk I thought he was serious.

(864): you looked like a weeble wobble. everytime we thought you were going to fall you bounced back up . . . you're an amazing drunk

(720): How did I get so drunk? We had to fish that girl out of the Goodwill Donation Box.

(502): i was drunk at family dinner telling about my gay brothers sex ads on craigs list

(323): Don't be mad at me. I know peeing in your drawer is 1 thing and peeing on you while you're sleeping is another, but im sorry..i love you

(817): stop leaving fruit for so long in the fridge. After you left she finished off the bottle of Jack and now she's petting your moldy orange and yelling us to get back so we don't take her Chia Pet away

(248): He kept trying to stuff the yorkshire terrier in his mouth. Poor thing looked terrified.

(214): She wanted to fuck you. You threw up on her. Congrats.

(509): I'm glad you talked me out of that flying penis tattoo.

(205): omg. weirdness. this guy just followed me 5 miles in a car to ask for my phone number. i think he would've gone farther but i pulled over and asked him what the fuck he was doing.
(1-205): well did you give him your number?
(205): haha yeah. i mean he worked so hard for it. . . .

(631): tequila mockingbird is the worst book i have ever read.
(1-631): don't you mean "to kill a mockingbird?"

(925): Gave great blow j. Lied to boss. Puked outside of car while doing drive of shame. Smoked a bowl. Fed boss another fib. Walked into fire hydrant. Welcome to fucking Monday morning.
(860): just wear a hood. you're not obligated to talk to anyone when you have a hood on.

(240): I think god invented the sun to punish me when i drink too much.

(914): Please tell me you agree that smokey the bear has the potential to be a scary serial killer

(306): I am whisper screaming to bohemian rhapsody in my cubicle . . . but I have no booze for the epic part so I chugged my coffee . . . not as epic

(281): Nice! Your little brother's first lesbian!

(610): Agreed. Platonic mer-men only.
(240): I dont think mer men have penises anyway where would it be? Theres no legs for it to go between
(610): I'm sure it works out somehow . . .

(707): Regardless, you never quit out of your internet. You left your porn on the living room comp. Then you passed out four feet from the chair with your hand still down your pants. We decided that we should go back to her place instead. Worlds best wingman.

(559): my dad came in to wish me a happy birthday and found me passed out in my underwear with the lights on and a plate of meat on the bed. i bet he was proud to have contributed to my creation in that moment

(515): took him home. told him i would rock his world. passed out. a for effort f for follow thru

(404): Not sure what happened last night, but there are four mini bikes outside and some guy is wearing my shirt passed out in the breakfast nook. Won't be telling the grand kids about this one.

(614): She said I could do whatever I wanted to her. I pumped for 20 seconds, apologized, rolled over and passed out. I sit directly across from her at work. Awkward?

(630): I passed out in the cab. Woke up to the cabby yelling SIR SIR WE ARE AT THE TRAIN STATION!! SIRRRR!!

(443): Please tell me I didn't pass out while we were having sex last night . . . and if so I am sooooo sorry.

(206): remember that time i ran away from the bar and passed out in a street cot?
(206): neither do i

(973): haha omg you stole $185 from a passed out drunk indian on your porch and called the ambulance??
(630): savin' lives aint cheap

(403): she said i have a nice penis, i told her only bob saget and god could judge that.

(306): Someone wrote that you're a whore in one of the bathroom stalls
(1-306): I didn't know I was popular enough to be hated. This is awesome

(418): I have nothing to say, just wanted ur phone to vibrate

(506): haha you were like: "I don't want to uh pressure you.." as you took your own shirt off

(514): i'm eating jello out of a teacup with a fork. awesome?

(586): If I don't wake up snuggled up to 14 ice cream sandwiches, my life is incomplete.

(709): I just thought you should know I puked up a penny.

(212): Dude, I was completely sober last night, didn't puke on my shoes, went home with an incredibly beautiful girl, wore a condom, and didn't wake up in a puddle of urine this morning.
(248): hah, sarcasm, classic

(804): I just woke up in bed with 4 girls. Either I dont remember the best night of my life or they think im gay.

(508): awoke with 47 plastic lawn flamingos in my bed and on surrounding floor. explanation?
(1-508): you said they were your minions of evil that protected you from ferrets.

(860): you left your sweatshirt here the night we had sex and you cried

(570): If the Four Horseman of the Apocalypse gang banged each other and had a kid, it would look like the creature I woke up next to this morning.

(859): We got drunk. You dropped your phone off a roof and began a relationship with a dog. Id say the night was a success.

(810): i woke up under my mattress pad with him laying naked next to me and his wwjd bracelet on my nightstand.
(1-810): nice, that's exactly what jesus would do.

(309): So I woke up in a guy's bed this morning, failed to hook up with him, then went home and masturbated. This is not the kind of independence I planned on celebrating today.

(512): Did yall have sex?
(214): Well we both woke up naked and there was a condom wrapper on the floor, but I don't remember so does that count?
(512): Def not . . . that's how I managed to keep my number under 10 for all of college- If you don't remember, it didn't happen

(479): Oh and ps. . . . i was sleeping soundly until i woke up by the sound of amy on the phone with her mom sobbing hysterically because she can't stop having the shits.

(202): I just woke up with no wallet,no shoes, and a bottle of OJ at the mall. This can't be good.

(907): I woke up this morning and thought "Im sure I've seen this house in a porno" and instantly googlemapped myself

(818): I woke up this morning with "guy in polar bear j.crew boxers" written on my stomach along with a 5 digit phone number . . .

(207): I just woke up with a girl who has left and right tattoed on her wrists. In french. I may need to stop drinking.

(208): I woke up this morning to the buzzer on my oven going off . . . I cooked fish sticks at 425 degrees for 5 hours last night. my house smells awesome

(901): You'll be OK if you get a pill. Don't freak. At least you didn't give head in an alley last night.

(216): dude i woke up to 20 missed calls from you, 3 from a blocked number and had 13 voicemails that all said "send me a picture of your tits."
(814): so im guessing thats a no.. . . .

(919): sunday funday is beginning to lead into maybe i should go to meetings Monday

(352): I just woke up and realized I puked in my boxers WTF.
(904): You stay classy.
(352): The worst part was I forgot until I tried to put them on.

(508): just woke up and my boobs have "fun police" written on them

(848): I fell asleep next to my cousin and woke up with my hand in her pants because i though it was lisa

(937): just found a nuva ring under the side of my bed. dont know what chick it came from. changing my name and moving to portugal.

(813): I slept walked to the toilet and woke up pooping. Easily one of the most disorienting events of my life.

(262): When I woke up his cat was sleeping on my face and i had scratch marks on my neck. not happy.
(612): only room for one pussy in that bed.

(703): Just woke up wearing a top hat and simpsons boxers. i also found more money in my wallet then what i had before going out, about $1000 more

(215): I woke up wearing no shirt sleeping next to a half-eaten grilled cheese.
(717): Well did you call the grilled cheese yet? Or r u waiting the usual 3 days?

(631): dude, i woke up naked in her front yard . . . apparently i tried to leave in the middle of the night, forgot my clothes and decided, "oh heres a nice patch of grass to sleep on" I think god is up there laughing at me.

(207): I blacked out in 45 minutes and woke up with a missed call from someone I saved in my phone as the karate kid.

(805): I just woke up to a guy kissing me goodbye and leaving for class. I don't know where I am, don't have any clothes on, my underwear are gone, and the shoes I found with my dress aren't mine. He just walked in and gave me my phone. I was on my period. Come get me I will walk to the nearest intersection and wait.

(813): dude i woke up laying next to some guy. i dont have my bra or his name. he has a nice tv though.

(480): allegedly i woke up at 5am sat in the dishwasher and peed

(919): So I guess I got home drunk last night and shaved my pubes. downside- I left a moustache over my dick

(203): I'm sorry for everything. i woke up with two citations stapled to my shirt.

(978): I woke up fully clothed on top of my sheets and i didnt even pee myself..so proud.

(781): I just woke up surrounded in unopened snacks

(415): Woke up this morning to a janitor hitting me in the head with his bucket in the hallway of my building. An alumni was next to me because we locked ourselves out of my room and couldn't figure out where my roommates were.

(210): i threw up in his kitchen sink and then used a measuring cup to drink water because i couldn't find a clean glass. i just threw up down the stairs. it's gonna be a long walk home.

(925): it's my fault, I passed out instead of getting up to pee.

(306): Thats not how I planned it, its just the way she passed out

(915): After I made out with her she fell asleep and started pooting in her sleep. Are we sure lesbians are hot? Cause that wasn't.

(856): I just fell asleep with a sandwich in my mouth at Cosi.. people definitely saw

(630): Britney fell asleep on the couch in the foyer, got up stripped then pissed on the floor. Then got dressed and went to sleep in it. Also downstairs toilet clogged. Not me. I will be gone by the time you get home from work. Have fun.

(805): Dude. I just woke up without a shirt or bra on. Apparently I fell asleep with a quesadilla in my mouth. I can feel my liver hating me.

(514): Please tell me you did not just serenade her with "Let's Get it On"?
(1-514): Yeah I think it worked. My penis thanks you, Captain Morgan.

(514): you want to go make fun of the strippers on try out night
(1-514): i got kicked out last time for laughing

(613): somehow on my way home with matt, I ended up straddling steve on the sidewalk and polling the people walking by on whether or not we should have sex.

(416): dude I just sharted for the first time ever, kind of gross
(647): well what did you think, shitting your pants would be fun

(419): just went to get groceries. a cashier said she saw me last night. i guess i carried a broom back from the party and swept the street the whole walk back . . . and i claimed to be in the cast of Wicked

(604): My feet smell like cheese. Makes me hungry.

(705): I think taking a nice shit is a lot more satisfying than an orgasm. This is probably why I'm single.

(604): there's paper in my vomit.

(843): Grinding on my ninth grade teacher. Dreams really do come true

(847): i took some ambien and I TRIPPED out . . .
i went into my mom's room to say goodnight and i
don't remember anything . . . she said that i got really
pissed at her because we were living in the Keebler
elf tree and she was visiting other trees, then i started
laughing hysterically and she goes "whats so funny?"
and i go "there are 7 people sitting on my knees" and
she goes "doesn't that hurt?" and i said "no we're
sitting in a bowl" and then i capped it off and said
"join the crazy train bro" and passed out.

(520): If I were a boy, I'd name my penis Reptar.

(775): before smithy murders me i need you to
know 3 things. 1) i got with smithy's
little sister last night. 2) i will always love you
like my own brother. 3) smithy's little sis digs
anal.

(978): Answer the phone when I call you in
a second. Just got pulled over for getting
road head, going to secretly put you on
speaker phone, this should be good

[SMELLS]:

(812): Rocking a Headband at the strip club, because of Rock of Love this shit is like their kryptonite, I smell like stripper butter and back child support.

(304): I smell stomach acid.

(631): If Ritalin and Plan B had an illegitimate child it would smell like me.

(508): he smells like the inside of heather mills' fake leg

(714): my room smells like sperm. sweet.

(678): Our house smells like week old pizza, beer cans, cigarettes, and depressing career tracks. . . . get lysol.

(630): My bed smells like naked
(414): Haha. At least it doesn't smell like herpes

(310): your room smells of hookers.
(904): And success

(585): She's 40ish and I couldn't wake her up with a stick of dynamite. My sheets are going to be covered in glitter lotion and smell like grape vodka and shattered dreams tomorrow.
(585): Aren't divorce parties fun?
(1-585): You and I have very different definitions of fun.

(256): My hair reeks of homosexuality.

(301): My hands smell like the metro—like jizz and awesome.

(TASTES):

(203): it tastes like there's a party in my mouth and everyone is throwing up

(901): Im bringing wine tonight. Its from a merlot from nashville. i bet it'll taste like infidelity and teenage pregnancy.

(401): my mouth tastes like poor choices

(678): What are you drinking?
(404): Shitty Coors light. OM NOM NOM TASTES LIKE HIGH SCHOOL

(540): i think 'regret' was last night's theme. i could taste it in my mouth and woke up next to it.

(918): She looked like cheddar but tasted like limburger . . .

(732): my mkouth tastes houw teh zoo smelllls

(814): I told him it tasted like his mom..needless to say we were asked to leave.

(321): My mouth tastes like defeat. Did he at least have money?

(970): Drinking non-alcoholic beer is like going down on your cousin.
(970): Sure it tastes the same, but it ain't right.

(239): I'm not even going to ask how you know what chlamydia tastes like.

[LOOKS]:

(480): she looked like the bat from fern gully.

(216): My Blind Date Arrived. She looks like something I'd draw with my left hand.

(570): His stupid grin looks like he's mid-ejaculation

(518): He looks like a mix between a retired piano teacher and a cat that just swallowed a sock.

(217): she looks like luggage that fell from a plane

(+44): What's everyones problem with my costume?!
(1+44): It looks like a unicorn came on your face.

(518): She looks like Robin Williams dressed as a frog.

(773): Bridesmaid dress fitting. I look like a Weeble and Michelle looks like Malibu Barbie. I have to keep reminding myself that she has herpes so really, the playing field is more level than it might initially seem.

(616): If he looks like a Gremlin DO NOT get him wet.

(410): He looks like Jesus, if Jesus had let himself go.

(954): You ever start fucking a girl and realize she kinda looks like your mom?

(404): My penis looks like a roll of pennies
(303): Oh. Ok. I get the hint.
(404): Like a roll of pennies where the paper got wet & then dried all wrinkly and weird..

(201): Smith looks like a guy that goes on a lot of first dates

(919): I think your mom looks like a breed of donkey and elephant, but her boobs are perfect

(250): She looked kinda like Mario Batali?

(603): not only are you not the girl i fell in love with, but from the looks of it, you ate her

(212): Dude she looked like Jerry Garcia's knuckles

(818): dude, i look like john mccains neck right now

(309): Her tattoo looked like she paid for it with blowjobs.

(TEQUILA):

(434): I dont remember anything after Tequila & Apple Juice. May have disovered the recipe for mental bleach.

> (250): do you remember how we all fit in that bathtub?
> (1-250): tequila

(425): i'm chasing tequila w mint flavored ice cream, phil's chasing it w cream cheese, bashar's chasing it w pickles . . . i think we all know who the winner is. . . .

(215): I think tequila should come with a little jiminy cricket

(518): Wow.. I was doing a mental check of my bank balance & I literally just said to myself: 'I have 27 dollars and a bottle of tequila til tuesday-ill be fine'

(212): ??? When I first met her at the bar, she told me she was 23. After I bought her 3 shots of tequila, she told me she was really only 21. When we went back to my house, she said she was really only 19. She's still sleeping next to me butt naked. I'm afraid if she opens her mouth again I could be looking at 10 years.

(860): How come every time I drink Tequilla I piss on my coffee table?
(203): Again?

(949): It helps if you take a shot of boiling hot tequila right before puking, little trick i learned

[VODKA]:

(404): Mmmm, vodka for breakfast

(978): it turns out vodka filled condoms arent that funny

(519): Passed out watching pirates of caribbean with vodka in hand. Woke up to jenna jameson, with vodka gone.

(501): fighting downstairs. join me tonight to hear their makeup sex. also, let's make skittles vodka.

(407): Dude, hurry and get over. I need a wingman. She is on her 6th vodka shot and her resident ugly friend is still sober

(443): So called my VP's house on Sunday drunk and told him that if he didn't hire me for the new position I would skull fuck his wife. They asked me to go home today. Thanks again Vodka

(209): just took a cab, driver just asked what i'd been drinking- i said vodka, he said "can't do vodka-drunk, it makes me feel like i'm giving birth to myself ... no comment

(207): things it involved: vodka, boy parts, possible photos of me on a cell phone. things it did NOT involve last night: my bra, his pants, and sobriety.

(253): Well for starters i'm drinking vodka out of a bell pepper.

[BEER]:

(904): the best thing about dollar beer night is beer is only a dollar.

(910): wow wtf my bar tab was 80 dollars
(910): IT WAS DOLLAR BEER NIGHT

(847): Why did you take off so early
(224): No more beer. And also. Threesome. Maybe. Ill let you know.

(231): we both passed out while playing beer pong, woke up in the morning and continued to play coffee pong to cure our hangovers

(415): Left my ID again and at a Giant's game. This is the second time they accepted my handgun safety certificate as proof of ID to buy beer.

(859): it's 4 am, i'm drinkin beer and re-drywalling my bathroom. this could possibly be a bad idea.

(570): She said I was really immature but whatever . . . oh by the way we just bought a toilet and turned it into a beer bong so come over

(937): Evryone should know as good as ramen noodle cooked in beer sounds . . . its not

(WINE):

(402): I used a bag of wine as a pillow last night.

(404): I saw that some person on TFLN used a bag of wine as a pillow. I tried it last night. I forgot to close the spout. I woke up and thought my face had a period

(770): We were so bored at work tonight that we were in dry storage taking turns pouring the boxed wine we use for cooking into each others' mouths. I think I'm starting to understand the "problem" aspect of "drinking problem."

(902): perhaps when you are drinking red wine from a tall glass with a straw it is time to call it a night

(509): I'm having a small glass of wine in the hopes that it will revive me. I think my liver just cried a little.

[WHATEVER IT TAKES]:

(571): final count. 18 beers. 4 shots baileys. 2 shots vodka. 1 glass champagne. vomited in the yard after losing my phone in a field for 8 hours. Possibly played tag with myself

[WHO DID IT BEST?]:

(714): we're chasing vodka with high fives

(201): I'm chasing vodka with french fries.

(503): we're chasing vodka with hard eggnog.
(971): In july?

(206): he was on top of me and all of a sudden stopped and starting picking his nose . . . i asked him if he was okay, he sort of looked confused, and he told me he had a booger that hurt. guess its a good thing i wasnt planning on dating this guy

(734): i was shrooming and she was sobbing. i was trying to be sympathetic, but i could see the veins working like worms under her skin. and then her face stripped down to the muscle.
(1-734): what was she crying about?
(734): i wanna say it was the lack of skin on her face but maybe she lost her job.

(847): i hate when u poo a lot and when u wipe theres no poopy residue on the TP. it makes me feel like my butt hole is hiding something from me. just had 2tell sum1.

(403): I'm seriously so bored I'm seeing how many rooms I can masturbate in before I get caught.
(403): Four. Poor grandma . . .

(860): Just got booed while taking a piss and asked if I 'call that a penis.' Get me the fuck out of yankee stadium.

(404): this morning my mom told me to get a new vibrator because mine was too loud last night
(404): i fell asleep watchin iron chef that was the blender she heard. i dont even own a vibrator

(613): she was so hammered she started drinking dishwasher detergent
(613): I dont know whats funnier—that, or that we learned that poison control is closed at 2 AM

(562): Whatever. They have the same name, so it's not even cheating. It's brand loyalty.

(908): girl in front of me in lecture is looking up on ask.com about chlamydia.

(604): I projectile vomited into my sink. Jealous?
(778): Kind of. My puke would have just dribbled down my chin and missed the sink completely.
(604): Ohh that happened after I started to cry.

(972): **i WaNt TO sLaP mY niECe wHO ThINks iT iS cUte tO WriTE LiKE tHiS**

(314): There's a woman at Starbucks that keeps pushing her stroller into me.
(818): Punch her baby.

(973): my 3 year old cousin just woke up screaming "IT WON'T GO DOWN!"

(404): In retrospect, pretending to punch a 9 year old girl in the face was a terrible analogy to use in a piano lesson.

(209): is it wrong to smoke out middle schoolers?
(1-209): yes . . . dear jesus what did you do?
(209): bwahaha. ask your little brother in about 20 minutes. im dropping him off.

(413): I just sold weed to a guy holding a baby . . . does this make me a bad person?

(812): So someone put the baby mannequins in sex positions

(340): just saw a prosititute with a baby stroller . . . question is . . . if the baby wakes up is the blow job free?

(707): I still think their baby is ugly. I also still think it's yours.

(201): When my kids ask how I lost my virginity Im going to have to tell them of a mythical thing called "Myspace" and how strangers could lure you into their "den of love" thanks to clever quotes and graphics

(313): So I hogged the stall at Denny's for so long that a little kid shit his pants and ran crying to his mother. Am I a terrible person for this being the proudest moment of my life?

(405): So tired and we had a cokehead in the salon today making us bleach her whole head because she thought it would let her pass her drug test for custody of her kid

(1-405): Oh.My.God.

(804): omg this kid i'm babysitting is making a penis out of playdough ahhhh.
(804): He just rolled me a 'baby penis' as opposed to his 'big boy' penis that he crafted . . . he just demanded that I roll him a penis.

(202): the stripper made me go home becuz she had to take her kid to a birthday party in the morning

(604): I hate you, and I hope you have babies soon that you love very much. Then I will steal them and feed them to sharks, and you will be so heart broken that you never want to have any more kids and you'll just hide out in a dark room all day wondering how someone could feed another persons babies to sharks.

(925): "Ever since I killed her kid she be actin' shady." Actual quote overheard at Marine World just now. Oh God.

(570): I woke up this morning in a strange bed with a kid with an accent playing with my feet.

(402): apparently, it's not a good idea to make jokes about sending newborns through airport security xrays. the moms dont see the humor.

(717): But why'd she put it on the conveyor then?

(785): I wonder what percentage of toys r us merch ultimately becomes a sex toy . . .

(1-785): In my case? 100%

206): Sometimes I get depressed that my son is too young to understand how hot his babysitter is.

(215): im as drunk as the barefoot contessa. GET TO MY LEVEL

(609): dude. stop pregaming the food network.

(570): If Billy Mays did an infomercial on your dick, it still wouldn't get you laid.

(818): i wonder what megan fox's vagina feels like.
(615): Heaven soaked bacon.

(973): Herpes is a lot like Arnold Schwartzenneger. Because it always comes back. Also, because it is usually in some way in control of California.

(612): I think tonya harding is in my dwi class!
(763): Ask her how she and Jeff Gillooly split the cats after the divorce.

(773): he's the Salvador Dali of pubic shaving

(970): i just realized Britney Spears and I are more alike than I thought. Both of us have our parents in complete control of our lives, we both have restraining orders on previous boyfriends, and we all know both of us can put on a hell of a show

(650): the night i cant remember will be the night i always remember thanks to my "i <3 spencer pratt" tattoo . . .

(850): paul mccartney is starting to look like angela lansbury

(512): I think I just was a dick to Paul Rudd.

(612): that's when I learned why R Kelly peed on that bitch

(540): you're like the Cesar Millan of boners . . . you understand them on a different level.

(540): Sometimes I think its so cool that a dick that has been inside kate moss has also been inside me. So exciting.

(941): I think that we as people have rights and that we should at the very least be warned before being subjected to Fergie

(845): If Curt Schilling could pitch a game with that blood-filled sock . . . if Tiger Woods won the 2008 US Open with a torn ligament, then I'd be an embarrassment to the human race if I couldn't manage to at least jerk him off even if I was still crying after he put it in my butt.

(813): I woke up (not at home) to find out I kissed Ryan Caberra, flashed for free gumbys and carried around an inflatable moose named Johnson. Great success.

(716): I just saw a dog and thought "Hey! A goat!" Then realized it was a dog. Now I'm sad.

(705): Fantastic night. drank beer from a wine bottle, danced on a van, chased a llama, and fell from a fence

(215): Sundresses, hats, and big glasses. That is the greatest trick the devil ever taught women.

(330): I don't know where I am but the food in the fridge is awesome.

(724): also, i may or may not be wearing a cape right now. hint: i am.

(314): he has a girlfriend so we used my stuffed animals to pretend to have sex

(970): I just remembered that last night when we tried to walk off the spins you said "pretend i'm your pet dinosaur" so i walked you around on an invisible leash while you made t-rex hissing noises.

(413): his facebook status quotes britney spears so there is always that

(201): I'm smoking weed out of a trumpet
(908): I just did a slip and slide down the hall way of my apartment building
(201): Tie

(513): Dude someone changed all the contacts in my phone to I Like Eggs

(717): Boobs are like coupons for free stuff

(512): Sometimes I wonder if my friend studies mystic Christian theology because he's afraid to come out of the closet. Evidently, it's okay to talk about God coming inside you, but not to say the same about dudes.

(323): Pride was great cause we really can now appreciate how far we've come as gay people!
(206): Doll, if you're still fucking strangers behind the WeHo Sonic while high on E then we've come as far as 2003 . . .

(561): At a straight bar and Poker Face just came on . . . must . . . resist . . . urge to gay it up
(915): Why would that come on at a straight bar? I thought they just played Don't Stop Believin and Wonderwall on repeat

(301): Fuck you I wanted that fabulous flaming homo to win american idol . . . its like we lost the gay marriage vote . . . again

(636): Well I'm going to a gay club in my banana suit. You should come. My bro is going as a pirate. I don't know if there's a theme.

(267): i voted against prop eight dipshit. more weddings = more CAKE.

(617): You're the unicorn of the gay community. Unbelievable and unattainable.

(313): Every time there's an awkward silence a gay baby is born

(516): I seem to have left my pride at pride

(609): Wow senior week shows you new things about yourself
(1-609): Is this the I'm gay speech?

(563): My dad just sent me a text telling me to "say hi to all the luscious bitches" at the gay bar. Guess this explains my childhood

(954): Dude, I don't think I'll ever be able to find a girl for me . . .
(1-954): Is this the gay conversation?

(416): If I don't come home tonight, I've died in a pile of gay.

(804): Gayer than 8 guys blowing 9 guys
(1-804): wow, that really makes you stop and think.

(917): I'm not really sure actually. until I fell in love with a boy (which was just a few weeks ago) I thought my attraction to men was purely physical.
(201): so you were gay . . . and then you realized you were EVEN MORE gay

(313): So its not gay if you have sex with another woman and its academic
(1-313): so what if I'm having sex with a woman for recreation?
(313): Thats gay

(708): We're gonna have to suck it up and start making out for free drinks. No homo. I'm watching Tyra "I kissed a girl and I got free drinks."
(1-708): Let's do it. All homo

(323): I totes stole your whore crown.

(239): With great power comes great responsibility.

(202): based on who turned up here tonight the whole evening should just be called "mistakes i made when i was fat"

(203): It was like a mary poppins bag, except a sexual mary poppins bag.

520): But I don't consider them one night stands. They're auditions.

(317): when im not freaking out about dying alone and unloved, i actually really enjoy being single

(+27): I really love her but I don't think I can go the rest of my life without anal.

(954): everyone is single if you try hard enough

(610): Just once id like a girl to say to me in the dracula voice, i want . . . to suck . . . your dick . . .

(504): That level of neurosis does not find love outside of Grey's Anatomy.

(516): Dating is not our generation's strong point. We're an era that's good at getting laid.

(206): would you consider dating someone with braces an investment

(858): Facials are how you say "I love you" in porn star.

(860): I'm in love with you.
(1-860): huh?
(860): Don't be nervous. I'm just saying—if you had a dick, I'd suck it.

(775): Just asked what her favorite part of a guys body is. She said ballsack. I'm in love.

(845): I missed Saved by the Bell this morning, but Ashley in a later episode of Fresh Prince is keeping the morning wood alive.

(805): My cousins just decided to make a catapult to spread my Grandpa's cremated remains. I love my family.

(909): It must have been true love
(604): I don't call true love eating a bag of doritos and then going down on each other

(267): Overheard: "his girlfriend fucks him with the lights off. It's not serious."

(716): lmfao. well really. it's not love if you cringe at the site of his anus.

(609): People in love make me want to vomit

(212): i hate this light. i wouldnt even hook up with me in this light

(518): Anthony wouldn't know good sex if it sat on his face

(703): Hey, what's Italian for "Oh dear, that wasn't supposed to happen yet"? It's pretty urgent

(651): nailed a girl as she was wearing a darth vader shirt. Cross that one off my list.

(801): Successfully pulled the houdini tonight. Check that off my list.

(832): i can now get sex on a playground off my list of things to do in life.

(443): Things on my life to do list: hold a pound of marijuana. Check

(321): well we can cross tagging a chick in a movie theatre off the list of things to do before we die

(510): I just saw a midget ride by on a scooter . . . wearing a bowtie and a helmet. My life is complete.

STEREOTYPE THE STATES

Alabama

(870): Only in Alabama do they play hymns in a bar!!!

Arizona

(480): God may have created the world in 7 days, but I can almost guarantee you that Satan himself is responsible for the creation of Arizona.

Arkansas

(615): arkansas has a gas station called kum and go. . . . story of my life

California

(760): i'm pretty sure the devil's penis is california-shaped

Colorado

(303): A joint and a Nerds Rope = breakfast of champions for the unemployed

Connecticut

(203): My day is ruined!
(212): Why, is little Miss Connecticut's tennis racket stuck in her beamer?
(203): . . . . Who told you?

Delaware

(215): At a bar where three women in denim shorts are debating techniques and skillsets for wrangling goats. You stay classy Delaware.

DC

(202): On Saturday, I sharted on my roommates dog while trying to make it smell my farts. Today I got security clearance to work for one of the most respected and secretive govt agencies in the US
(703): It's the American dream

Florida

(407): You're the only person with a favorite bar in Disneyworld

Georgia

(484): I was in a gas station that sold tazers and I just saw a billboard that said "Strippers, need we say more?" God I love Georgia!

Hawaii

(312): How the fuck did we find Hawaii, let alone make it a state?.

Idaho

(303): How's Idaho?
(720): Fat.

Illinois

(847): I just want you to know that me val and amanda are drinking on top of a hill lookig at the chicago skyline drinking icehouse and we just peed in public.

Indiana

(502): You need anything in Indiana?
(502): Maybe some meth?

Iowa

(952): I saw a sign that said World's Largest Frying Pan next exit. Way to do your fucking part Iowa.

Kansas

(678): Actually overhead in the Wichita airport: "I'd trade my ovaries for a 40"
(770): Kansas rulz

Kentucky

(513): i just won a 100 dollar gift card to walmart in a karaoke contest . . . i love kentucky

Maine

(207): The mall is playing a fucking country mix of Lady Marmalade.
(207): welcome to maine.

Maryland

(202): I am apparently in rockville maryland. I just threw up my tater tots I had fro brunch in a safeway parking lot. Then ordered a pizza. Pepperoni and pineapple. I'm sitting in the parking lot, next to my barf, waiting for my pizza. WOOF. Someone just gave me an oxycontin tab. Can u come get me? I'm scared

Massachusetts

(401): how is it that boston is so bitchin and the rest of massachusetts sucks so much?
(617): how is it that you still think "bitchin" is an acceptable term anymore?

Michigan

(616): GM filed for bankruptcy, all the dealerships closed, and it's june and I'm in jeans and a sweatshirt and I'm cold. What is the point of living in this state anymore?

Minnesota

(703): the dancing wasn't as good as i thought it would be

(1-703): Well theyre all white AND from minnesota . . . I mean they were working with what they had

Mississippi

(540): just saw a sign on a trailer home that said i'm beautiful, single, and affordable! God i'm going to miss mississippi!

Missouri

(805): bar tonight had a doorbell to get in and last night i saw my neighbors fuck on the balcony, she wore a nurse outfit. Missouri isn't so bad . . .

Montana

(406): Only in Montana can you find Septic Services that would display "Christian owned and operated" on the side of the truck. I'm oddly going to miss this state.

Nebraska

(402): i just saw a man dusting the fake palm trees at the mall
(402): . . . welcome to nebraska

Nevada

(416): Dude I need you to do me a solid.
(416): Google 'annulment' and send me what ever you find.

New Hampshire

(603): New Hampshire has cheap booze, hockey and looks like it's 69ing with Vermont . . . yeah, that's about it.

New Jersey

(484): Jersey . . . The gateway drug of america.

New Mexico

(832): There are so many mexicans in new mexico they have the white people do THEIR lawns

New York

(631): peeing in bathroom at penn station and the homeless man next to me is combing his beard with a fork . . . god I love new york

North Carolina

(336): If this place produced love children they would be born wearing Lilly Pulitzer with raging coke addictions.

North Dakota

(701): I'm so bored at work
(215): you work for a company that involves telling people about North Dakota . . . what did you expect exactly?

Ohio

(724): Ohio: like a prepubescent girl, flat and unfulfilling.

Oklahoma

(405): I have a client coming in and there's a note that says she wants her hair to look like Elisabeth Hasselback's from The View
(1-405): that's Oklahoma for you

Oregon

(415): u know ur in oregon when the cop tells u to keep the beer cans he made u pour out so u can recycle them

Pennsylvania

(717): I had to do the walk of shame barefoot on a partially dirt road. I love hooking up in rural pennsylvania.

Rhode Island

(412): In Rhode Island you can strip when you're 16 if you're home by 1130
(401): I love my state.

South Carolina

(845): I just saw a gas station that was boarded up and turned into a strip club. . . . gotta love South Carolina

South Dakota

(605): I'm towing my little brother down the road on a sixty year old tractor, we're taking up the whole highway, and no one cares. I love South Dakota.

Tennessee

(801): Yah man, that place is surreal
(731): Man, I'm from Tennessee. What the fuck is surreal?

Texas

(518): everything is bigger in texas. Including my drinking problem.

Utah

(619): Moving to Utah. Got sick of alcohol and have a severe wife shortage.

Vermont

(207): Vermont's license plate should be "the way life should be". Maine doesn't have weed like this!

Virginia

(703): Just stopped in a Walmart to take a piss. There is an empty heineken bottle beside the urinal. You stay classy Virginia.

Washington

(206): I think we should urban dictionary "drive of shame." It involves a sprint to your car in his underwear and shirt, surreptitiously trying to put on your bra on at stoplights without attracting attention from neighboring cars, and lurking in your car a block from home so you can know when your roommate leaves for work.

West Virginia

(304): this other lifeguard and I are actually considering paying a kid to shit in the pool

Wisconsin

(920): Dude wearing an actual packer helmet, packer jacket and packer clogs riding a harley. I love Wisconsin.

Wyoming

(973): I just saw someone get breathalyzed on horseback . . . I love Wyoming.

THX

LL:
Thanks to: Brandon, Patrick, Erin,
Philip Bobby.
Sorry to: My parents.

BB:
Mom and Dad.
My brother, Robert Billions, and his
personal assistant, Philip Bobby.
Lauren, Mark, Ryan, Brandon, David,
and Todd.
ESK and 8449 for supplying my west
coast office.
Erin and Patrick for making books
of things that already appear on the
Internet.
The Internet for allowing people to
think Lauren and I are funny.